Curious Events Occurred
ON THE WAY
TO MY FUNERAL

A Retired Journalist's Report on his Earth Odyssey
Plus Encounters with Both Known and Unknown Worlds

John S M Smith Nov. 2019

By John S. M. Smith

Keep up the good work folks!! ♡ JS

Curious Events Occurred
ON THE WAY
TO MY FUNERAL

A Retired Journalist's Report on his Earth Odyssey
Plus Encounters with Both Known and Unknown Worlds

ISBN # 9781699263259
Library of Congress # 2019912587

Published by Crow Farm Books
Printed by Kindle Direct Publishing

Also available through Amazon:
The Crow Farm Cookbook:
A Manual of Food & Hospitality
with Stories & Other Entertainment
by
Catherine & John Smith
(Second Edition ©2010)

Cover photo:
The author with his two favorite sticks
near Moose, Wyoming on the Snake River.
Photographed by his Aunt Betsy Cowles.

Dedicated to Harper G. Brown
Who devoted his life to making the lamps of the lost
burn a little brighter.
(1906-1985)

Preface

There were several objects of interest on our mantelpiece in Kentucky where I grew up. There was an ancient club called a shillelagh that belonged to an ancestor in Ireland. It had been hewn from a single, gnarly root and had probably been used either for self-defense or to cripple a marauding creature, or perhaps both. We have no idea what life was like for the ancestor who wielded that shillelagh.

Also on the mantle were a pair of drumsticks and a sword. Both belonged to a relative who fought for the North in our Civil War. He enlisted as a "drummer boy" because he was too young to be a soldier. When old enough to join the fight, he saw action in the Battle of Bull Run, Shiloh and several other campaigns. He ended up a captain in the Union Army wearing the same sword that rested on our mantle. Sadly, he left no record of his experiences in the war, the devastation that he had witnessed or his thoughts after returning to life in Louisville after the Civil War.

I have often felt a sense of loss when relatives I never knew failed to leave a record of who they were, what they were thinking, or what they experienced in their time on Earth. So I am hoping to set an example for others in hopes that they might be willing to leave their stories for those who follow.

Parts of my own life story may puzzle you, because they border on the "irrational." The truth is, I have been either blessed with, or cursed by, what I call "curious events." These events I have absolutely experienced, yet have no way of explaining either to myself or to others. Is there a problem with that? Yes. Some "other worldly stories" may be threatening to another person's belief system. And, since we don't want to be guilty of that, it is best to simply warn readers to Please Proceed At Your Own Risk.

Table of Contents

Chapter 1
The Early Years

The Ohio River from the Louisville, Kentucky waterfront.
Our youthful efforts to float down to New Orleans on a rickety raft
always ended long before we reached the bridges of Louisville.

Life was fairly simple in the 1930s and 1940s. (I was born in 1933.) One could drink out of streams without getting sick and hitchhike without fear of being abducted. One could also "play hooky" from school with little chance of being reported to your parents. I was a fairly free spirit in those days, but when I exhibited too much exuberance, I would be spanked and sent to my room. That put me on the second floor of the old carriage house where we lived on my great aunt's property on the outskirts of Louisville, Kentucky.

After the usual tears and a brief period of feeling sorry for myself, I would take down the clothesline hanging in my closet, tie one end to the iron railing outside my window, and lower myself to the ground to spend the afternoon playing with my friends down the lane. Fortunately for me, no one ever seemed to notice that I was gone. Or, perhaps my parents simply didn't know what to do with me.

There was one other escape strategy that proved effective in my early school years in Kentucky. Barry Bingham was a pal of mine in the elementary grades at Ballard School. Ballard was a rural public school that closed its doors whenever the Ohio River jumped its banks and flooded the valley.

Barry and I, and a few others, shared a preference for the outdoors and freedom to explore the natural world rather than endure enforced classroom attendance. Barry's nose turned out to be the only dependable key to our freedom. When classroom boredom seemed unbearable, we would urge Barry to take a sacrificial swipe at his nose as he had done several times in the past. The result was always an impressive flow of red blood. We would rush to Barry's aid, shout to the teacher about this sudden emergency, and together we would gather up our heroic friend and rush him out the door toward the office. Toward the office, but never *to* the office! At the stairs we would change course and bolt for the front door and freedom. The afternoon would be spent catching frogs and looking in the creek for crawdads. We were never captured or disciplined. We never considered the possibility that our teacher might be overjoyed to have us gone for the day.

There was always a sense of adventure for those of us living not far from the Ohio River, because the spirit of Tom Sawyer and Huck Finn lived deep within us. On my daily bicycle ride to school up River Road, alongside the Ohio, I would watch the paddlewheels on the big boats as they churned against the currents, headed for Cincinnati and beyond. I knew that many years ago Mark Twain, aka Samuel Clemens, knew every turn of the Ohio River as he steered the giant riverboats upstream.

When we were a bit older, my friends and I would occasionally meet near the river's edge, drag logs out of the nearby woods and lash them together to form a makeshift raft in the spirit of Mark Twain, then shove off full of hope and excitement, bound for New Orleans a thousand miles away. However, by the time we got our half-submerged raft into the current and had finished eating the lunches our mothers had made for us, we began to have misgivings about our plan.

I have no recollection of how or when we got back to land or what became of our makeshift raft, but our hunger for adventure seemed totally fulfilled with each unsuccessful attempt we made to reach New Orleans.

When our country entered the Second World War, my father, a lawyer, enlisted in the Army Air Force and was sent to an assignment on the East Coast. Our family followed and rented a house in Milburn, New Jersey. From there my father commuted daily to an office in New York City.

Thinking back on it, I realize that I did not lose that need for adventure when I left Kentucky. I found myself in a new school, but there was no Ohio River in New Jersey. What to do? I found at least one adventurous lad in school. His name was Peewee Swain. I suggested that Peewee start saving quarters for a secret adventure that I had in mind.

A few weeks later Peewee and I met very early one the morning, walked a mile down to the Lackawanna Railway station in Milburn, took a commuter train to Hoboken, walked to the Staten Island Ferry Terminal and took a boat to Manhattan Island. We found a bus that dropped us off at Chinatown. It was like visiting another country. We spent most of the morning walking the streets and looking into shops, fascinated by the people, their different language and clothing. Eventually one man asked us why we weren't in school. "School? Oh, my, we must be late!" We located a bus, then the ferry and a train to the Milburn station, followed by the long walk home.

A few weeks after our successful outing, my mother was cleaning the basement of our house. She asked me where "this odd pile of things" had come from. "What things?" I asked. "This Chinese newspaper, and these coins with square holes in them, and the ceramic spoon-like objects with strange designs." "Ah, those must have come from Chinatown," I replied.

When World War II was over, my father was discharged and our family moved back to Kentucky. I returned to the public school in rural Jefferson County, Kentucky. Shocking for both me, and my parents, was the fact that the school required me, as well as my friend Steve Lord, to repeat the sixth grade. Somehow both Steve and I eventually managed to overcome our dyslexia to become fairly successful journalists.

Looking back on my elementary school years at Ballard School, I can't say that I learned a great deal, but I do have two indelible memories from that time. The first is standing in line on a chilly winter morning as the American flag was slowly raised – too slowly, I might add – while we made a pledge that went something like this: "We pledge allegiance to the flag and to the United States of America, one nation (*under God* was inserted in 1954) with liberty and justice for (*almost?*) all."

One saving grace for me at school was the presence of a remarkable man who was neither the principal nor a teacher. He was undoubtedly the lowest paid and lowest ranked adult at the school. His name was Ernest and he was the janitor. He was African-American, probably the grandson of a former slave. Without exception, all the students in the school, including myself, were White.

I have a clear memory of Ernest as a thoughtful individual with a soul as pure as spring water. He went about his work quietly at the school and without realizing it, his very presence probably touched the lives of everyone who crossed his path. If anyone deserves a memorial plaque for service to Ballard School, it should be Ernest.

Here are two stories about of my early days with my mother's remarkable sister, my Aunt Betsy. She lived in Colorado Springs not far from the Garden of the Gods. That was her favorite climbing spot where she often taught local children about rock climbing. Betsy was a delight to be with. She had climbed every peak over 14,000 feet in Colorado, and was the only woman on the 1950 American expedition seeking a safe route up Mount Everest. That was three years before the world's highest mountain was "conquered" by Sir Edmund Hillary and his guide Sherpa Tensing Norgay.

Aunt Betsy was also a high achiever when it came to snitching my dessert, an event that occurred quite often. "Johnny," Betsy would say, "see that eagle flying over the river?" My glance away from my lunch was enough for my aunt to artfully transfer the rest of my apple pie from my plate to hers.

At a very young age, Aunt Betsy took me on a private tour of the fascinating geysers and hot pools of Yellowstone National Park. I say private because at that early date there were few Park Rangers, few rules and almost no other tourists, so the two of us had the run of the place.

Betsy couldn't wait to show me how useful those steaming geysers could be. "Be a good boy, Johnny, and give me your shirt." She sent my dirty shirt down the gurgling hole along with tons of boiling water. We waited patiently near the geyser for the return of a clean shirt. Lots of boiling water came up, but no shirt. "Let's try your shorts, Johnny." Same result. I was down to my socks and underpants when we gave up. I have often wondered what was reported when a child's boiled clothes were discovered near a geyser with no sign of a boiled boy.

Aunt Betsy Cowles, mountaineer, photographer,
and the only woman on the American Expedition
to climb Mt. Everest in 1950.

Here is one more story about Aunt Betsy. This one involves my broken contract with God. I was maybe seven or eight years old, sitting in the snow with my back against a sharp rock shelf. Below me the glistening snow pack dropped off quickly, out of sight. I was alone on a steep mountainside in the Tetons of Wyoming and I knew what would happen to me if I stood up and lost my balance. I would pitch forward, slide right down the icy slope and drop onto the rocks hundreds of feet below.

The rest of the climbing party had moved on. They had been traveling upward, single file in the snow, talking excitedly about their climb plus whatever adults talk about. But they had failed to rope up or to remember that little Johnny had been quietly following behind.

That was when I contacted God for the first time. I told God that if he would just get me out of this fix, I would be a good boy from then on. Just then I heard someone calling my name. Around the outcropping came the rescue party, Aunt Betsy, my father, and their climbing friends.

The point of this story is not about climbing, it is about calling for help. And this you should know. After his rescue, Little Johnny forgot all about his pledge to "be a good boy," and whether or not God remembered Little Johnny's pledge still remains an unanswered question.

Enough about early childhood. It is time to move on to more puzzling subjects, like how one can avoid education while attending school.

Chapter 2
My Fruitless Pursuit of an Education

After my return to public school in Kentucky, my parents believed that my only hope of ever "achieving a decent education" was sending me away to boarding school in the East, which reportedly had helped others in my situation. In my first spelling test at the new school I was awarded a grade somewhere below zero percent, if indeed there is such a grade. That grade was due to points being subtracted for each misspelled word. Thus my total had traveled way below zero. Obviously, there was room for improvement.

Actually my only achievement at that school occurred when the faculty of the all-male boarding school felt the desire to inform us about human reproductive matters, meaning Sex Education. A special assembly was scheduled. Male faculty members and their wives sat on chairs in the large room, while we (male) students sat on the floor. The headmaster began by explaining how babies were formed. Specifically, he explained that thousands of sperm from the male proceed up through the female cervix to the uterus where the winning sperm finds and fertilizes the egg that has dropped down the fallopian tube. The result is the fetus, which becomes the child.

At the end of his brief talk, the headmaster asked if there were any questions. Since there were none, I raised my hand to find out what I considered an obvious omission in the presentation. "If only one of the thousands of sperm fertilizes the female's egg," I asked, "what happens to the other thousands of sperm?" There was complete silence from the faculty, their wives, as well as the headmaster. They sat there for a few moments, seemingly dumbstruck. Then they filed out silently without even answering my question. I concluded that the faculty really didn't know very much about reproduction. Of course, neither did we students.

Chapter 3
On to the Nationals

Capturing the half-mile in Madison Square Garden.
Unknown New York newspaper photographer.

Further on in my educational quest, I was enrolled in what is called a preparatory school in New Jersey, which is designed to prepare one for college. This meant three more years of schooling. (No one seemed to know anything about *dyslexia*, which I later learned was inherited from my very wise mother.) Those years might have been lost on me except for my discovery of a sport called Track. The truth is, I loved to run. Growing up in Kentucky, I had spent my childhood running up hills and down, whenever I could avoid walking. Walking took more time, was boring and no fun at all.

On my second year at that school, Bob Wallace, our admired, taciturn track coach, took us for the first time to the National Indoor Track Championship at New York City's Madison Square Garden. I had never been in a big track meet, so I was surprised when our coach told me that he had entered me in the half-mile race, a distance I had never before run, not even in practice.

The "Nationals" were a three ring circus of pole vaulting, shot put, hurdles, sprints, relays, long distance runs, javelin throwing, etc. When the half-mile was announced I lined up behind rows of other runners and took off when the starting gun sounded. We pounded around the wooden track in our spiked shoes like everyone else and jockeyed for space on the turns. The gun fired once more to tell us there was one lap to go. Then it was time for a sprint toward the finish line. I didn't really remember anything after that, it all happened too fast. But a press photographer from a New York newspaper was at the finish line and captured four runners in a tight row lunging for the tape. There was the well-known giant Thorgeson in the foreground, Kirk, feisty and fast, was on the far side, and somewhere in the middle, in first place with most of the tape across his chest, was the unknown upstart named John Smith.

The following year Smith won the half-mile again at the Garden, but he reports that he was alone at the finish line, and found it less than exciting. No photo finish, just a race against the clock. (Smith reported his best time for the half-mile on an outdoor track was 1:57)

After that, Smith hung up his track shoes and headed back to Kentucky. He said it was no fun being first, because it's just running in circles and winning doesn't really change anything anyway.

Robert Waters, on tractor, was my rough
and ready farm boss at Locust Grove.

Robert's older brother Duquet handled
the chickens, pigs and light chores
due to a heart condition.

Chapter 4
A Touchstone for Life

I believe that everyone has the recollection of some important time or place in childhood that is a touchstone for existence in later life. It could be a book, a person, a place, a song or an unusual event or experience.

For me, it was spending summers in Kentucky working with the Waters family on their timeworn farm named Locust Grove. That became my second home during my teenage years.

Life was a long struggle for the Waters' survival on the farm. The work was endless. It began with milking at 4 a.m. for Robert, and ended long after dark. Robert was the only person physically capable of working the hundred or so acres of Kentucky farmland. Duquet, Robert's older brother, helped when he could, but a weak heart kept him from the hardest farm work. Duquet's wife Elizabeth tended the garden, raised chickens and pigs, prepared meals and cared for an aging mother. When the strain of age, illness and taxes were too much, the farm was sold to Jefferson County, and the old farmhouse became a historic home. That was a long time ago. Since then those productive fields have been replaced by dozens of elegant houses. The old farmhouse, now a fully restored historic home, is visited by thousands of people each year to view the last home of George Rogers Clark, the American Revolutionary General who died at Locust Grove in 1818.

I often worked in the fields with Robert. He was as gruff as he was large, and together we harvested wheat and put up hay for his cows.

Robert would pull the old combine with a Case tractor while I rode the swaying combine binding the burlap sacks closed after they were filled with grain. Then I would pull an iron lever and watch the heavy bags slide down the shoot onto the field below. Every few hours Robert would throttle down the tractor, let the wheels and noise subside and the dust settle. With me following, Robert, who suffered from rheumatism, would limp over to the shaded fence and dig around in the grass for his water jug. It was always wrapped in a damp piece of burlap to keep the contents cool. Robert and I would sit on the ground in congenial silence as we drank from the jug that always carried the tang of Robert's chewing tobacco.

Other summers I spent working in the Wyoming oil fields or in the wilds of Canada as a fishing guide with my friend Norton Clay. I liked working out in the world. It was always an adventure.

With my dog Walt Whitman and good friend Norton Clay.
We were guides at Beauchene, a summer fishing camp
in Ontario, Canada. Unknown photographer.

Chapter 5
The Basics of Basic Training

Back to the future: After a lackluster senior year at the preparatory school plus being turned down by my college of choice, I faced an uncertain future. This was compounded when I dropped out as a freshman at the University of Colorado. What to do? The possibilities were endless, so I settled on fulfilling my obligation to the military and volunteered for the draft.

The main mission of Basic Training seems to be to turn a civilian individual into something like a military robot, someone who will follow orders without question. This posed a problem for someone as stubborn as me. Two things went wrong for the Army's basic training program while I was at Fort Knox, Kentucky. First, they made a mistake by selecting a "gung ho" John Smith as platoon leader. Second, they didn't discover until the last day of training that there was a second trainee by the same name. I was that second trainee, and definitely not gung ho! The result of that oversight is that I existed totally under the radar for the entire six weeks: no kitchen duty, no guard duty, fortunately no identity at all in the shadow of our platoon leader, the other John Smith.

I had a string of successes in "basic." On bivouac during night attacks in the snow, I discovered the value of generosity by giving away my ammunition to those eager to fire their rifles. Our rifles fired blanks, of course, but blanks fouled rifles mightily and that made it almost impossible to properly clean the weapons for inspection later that night. My rifle stayed clean, and I slept well. Others enjoyed firing their rifles, but paid dearly at inspection time.

During bayonet training, the instructor encouraged us to augment our bayonet lunges with manly grunts and unseemly utterances. It took little prompting to create a frightening chorus of wild banshees, snarling tigers, and bellowing bulls during our first practice. The instructor, totally disgusted by our antics, stomped away, never to return.

Weeks later, during our early morning march to "wire school," we noticed the long line of officers driving to work. Someone (it certainly wasn't me) encouraged marchers to feign various leg and other injuries as we marched down the road. We felt this would benefit the commuting officers by livening up their morning drive. A few days later we were assembled by our commanding officer. He reported dozens of complaints from drivers. NOW WHAT THE HELL IS GOING ON HERE? he demanded.

On weekends we were restricted to the base. However, yours truly, occasionally a master of escape, managed more than once on the weekends to leave the base for home in the trunk of a car. And that was how I happened to be in Louisville, in the busy kitchen at Locust Grove that Sunday, when there was a knock at the door. Duquet was operating the milk separator, Elizabeth was cooking lunch, and Robert was pinning up bills on the kitchen laundry line. "Can you get that, John?" Robert asked. I went to the door, opened it, and I was suddenly face to face with an Army officer bearing a row of gold stars on his uniform. It was Duquet and Robert's brother, General William Waters. I left the house as quickly as possible with visions of a military stockade in my head.

Chapter 6
Life after Basic Training

After Basic Training, I considered myself almost a normal soldier. I was assigned to serve in the defense of our nation's capital, then protected, not by flying *sneakers*, but by a ring of Nike anti-aircraft missiles, named after the Greek goddess of Victory. I was stationed at the headquarters company of that complex and was assigned to operate the company switchboard. I will back up a bit here and explain that I was assigned to the company switchboard because I had attended the wire school at Fort Knox. I have two confessions to make. First, I missed many of the lectures at wire school because I noticed that the soldiers who fell asleep in class were quickly identified and rudely awakened because they allowed their chins to fall on their chests resulting in dire warnings about sleeping on the job. On the other hand, having noticed this, I rolled up my cap, tucked it firmly under my chin to avoid a telltale head roll, and slept undetected through most of the lectures.

Now back to my assigned switchboard in Washington D.C. Things worked fine at first, until the afternoon when things slowed down and I felt sleepy. I rolled up my cap, stuck it firmly under my chin and sat up confidently at the switchboard. With my eyes closed while napping, I failed to see the red light on the switchboard. That was the commanding officer's phone. It was blinking and I was napping. Big Mistake. GET THAT NEW MAN OUT OF THERE! That was the commander's way of solving the problem. And it was not too long before I was on my way for reassignment to England.

The way a soldier gets from North America to England is through the "Pipeline," which means you are sent to a debarkation point on the coast and housed there until a ship arrives to take you to your destination. That could take a few days or a week or more. While awaiting a ship, one is often at the mercy of any work requirements needed at the debarkation point. So, it was no surprise when the door of our Quonset hut flew open one morning and a Sergeant greeted us with an order: EVERYONE ON YOUR FEET, FORM A SINGLE LINE AND FOLLOW ME TO THE MESS HALL FOR K.P. DUTY!

Like the good soldier that I was, I tied up my boots, got in line and headed out the door. On the way, I recalled a lecture we were given in basic training. We were instructed that when captured, the best opportunity to escape is soon after your capture rather than later, when you are deeper into enemy territory.

So, what's a poor captive to do? During a right turn toward the kitchen I dove into a nearby dumpster and spent the rest of the day playing pool in a recreation room. The next day I was loaded aboard a ship bound for England. It was then that I decided it was time to make amends for my unseemly disappearance on the way to kitchen duty. Once safely onboard, I asked an officer the following: "If there is a Chaplain onboard, I would like to volunteer my services." I was assigned the enviable job of overseeing the ship's library on the ship's well appointed top floor and talking with the lovely mothers and their excited children who were headed to England to meet their officer husbands and fathers. It was a cushy job that I didn't deserve, but I enjoyed my voyage hugely. It is very helpful to know when to volunteer.

Chapter 7
My Private Meeting with Darth Vader

I had no idea that Darth Vader lived in England. But it was no surprise considering the constant bombing, the fatalities and damage the British sustained during World War II. The landscape in England was bleak and so was the mood. When I was there in the early 1950s, I was assigned to the headquarters company of a missile defense system at an RAF base called Brize Norton, about an hour west of London. This was during the Cold War with Russia when our Strategic Air Command was sending regular reconnaissance patrols over Europe from our base in England.

As soon as I arrived at headquarters, I found my way to the personnel office, set down my duffle bag and asked a clerk if they knew of any openings. In fact they did. "Information and Education could use a man," the clerk reported. That sounded better to me than motor pool or kitchen duty, so I asked them to please sign me up.

Our office was in a small Quonset hut amid two solid blocks of larger huts. The office had two desks, one for Corporal Joseph Kropineki and one for me. Joe, from the coal-mining region of Pennsylvania, had somehow gained control over excess coffee beans on the base, so we always had fresh coffee brewing and were seldom without company.

Private First Class Smith and office mate Corporal Joseph Kropineki at an RAF base in England. Unknown photographer.

I wrote occasional articles for our battalion newsletter and gave uninspired monthly talks about military matters to bored recruits.

These talks were based on printed material sent from stateside, which were always earnest, and occasionally thoughtful.

Amazingly, the only blemish on my sterling military record was the time I refused to give a talk about "Combat." This being peace time, I had never been in combat and did not pretend to know anything about it. For my refusal, I was demoted to private first class, which of course, I fully deserved. Justice is indeed swift in the military, and the crime of not obeying an order is no laughing matter.

Now for my Darth Vader moment. It was a normal day at the RAF base. I was assigned to latrine duty that morning, so I left our small office and headed down a cement walkway toward my destination. I was about to turn left onto a second walkway when I abruptly stopped in my tracks. Directly ahead, and facing me, was a figure clothed in black. It was definitely Male, and he clearly had a message for me. Incidentally, I have labeled him Darth Vader for the purpose of making him more recognizable to you, and less frightening. Darth was earnest but not at all scary, and I was not afraid of him. Darth lacked the electronic voice box of the Star Wars
Darth, but he did have a strong, quiet presence. One might even call this sighting of mine an "apparition."

Darth and I seemed to communicate by telepathy, which was new to me. Our "conversation" went something like this: "Oh, you're Death, aren't you?" Answer: "Yes." Question: "And I will see you again sometime, won't I?" Answer: "Yes". Then he was gone. I turned left, found the latrine and got to work without thinking much about what had just occurred.

However, I did notice a difference in my outlook after that. It slowly dawned on me that Darth was delivering me the message that I was actually Mortal! Meaning that if I ever wanted to get anywhere, I had better get serious about life while my clock was still ticking. I signed up for a typing class and soon was appointed company clerk by our fine commanding officer, Captain Detweiler.

A few thoughts about my life in the military: I was clearly a non-conformist for much of my time in the Army, in part because it was peacetime. What if it had been in wartime? I can't answer that in the abstract. (Full disclosure: I am embarrassed to admit that I once earned the status of "Expert Rifleman" from the now infamous National Rifle Association.)

I know that many people have given their lives for others in wartime. But it is also true that wars have not always been the answer to solving the world's many problems. The truth is I don't know if I could, in good conscience, kill another person even if it was for a "good cause."

When my two years in the army were up, a troop ship carried me back to the states. As we approached New York Harbor, I recall the inspiring sight of the Statue of Liberty as we passed close by. Docking, I was amazed by the bright, floral colors of the shiny new American cars, so different from drab vehicles we saw in bomb-battered England.

Back home in Kentucky, I visited my dear sister Rachel. She had one bit of advice for me: "John, you now need to go to a really good university and get a good education." Some part of me must have realized that my sister was correct. It also dawned on me that most of my previous decisions about schooling had been made by my parents, rather than by myself.

With dear Sister Rachel and my dog Fritzi.
Photographed by Stuey Emerson.

I applied to only one university, the one that had turned me down years earlier. Their admissions department suggested I attend a local college and earn some respectable grades, then apply again. In Louisville I immersed myself in Walt Whitman and U.S. History, got decent grades and was finally accepted as a returning veteran on the

G.I. bill by the very-patient university that decided to give me another chance.

Three years later, after traveling east again and taking every course that interested me, including several with the incredible Art Historian Vincent Scully plus the dreaded Daily Themes, I graduated from the educational institution of my choice. (I nicknamed the university "Snail" because it took me so long to matriculate.) At graduation, which I ducked, I left behind a dozen fine friends plus a dachshund named Low-Life who belonged to the Chaplain. That's what happens when you move on in life.

Chapter 8
Seeking the Impossible – A Job

Bil Dunaway shaving at dawn before our climbing adventure
in Utah. He was the publisher of The Aspen Times
who gave me my first job as a reporter.

How do you gain "experience as a reporter" if no one will hire you? That was my dilemma when searching for my first newspaper job. My search was further complicated by the fact that in 1959 a national wire service had just gone bottom up and many experienced journalists were also looking for work.

When my hopes were flattened by reality, I turned to things familiar. I visited the old mining town of Aspen, Colorado, where I had often stayed while climbing with my mountaineering Aunt Betsy. In nearby Woody Creek, I quickly found a job in the fields harvesting hay. A few weeks later I visited the local *Aspen Times* office and talked with the owner, Bil Dunaway. It turned out that Bil (he spelled his name this way) was planning to launch a new weekly newspaper downriver in Glenwood Springs. He was brave enough to put me to work on the project. We called the new publication *The Glenwood Sage*, and with the help of Joe Koeller, an experienced advertising man, we were in business.

Soon after launching *The Sage*, I married Katy Sterling, a talented math teacher in the Aspen school system who hailed from Cooperstown, New York. The two of us soon moved into a modest log cabin on the outskirts of Glenwood Springs. Life was indeed moving rapidly! Finishing college, finding a job, getting married, all in one year. What more could a fellow want? Actually, plenty. After a year of working on a weekly newspaper, I realized that I had much more to learn about the newspaper world. So the two of us packed up and headed for my hometown, Louisville, Kentucky, a city with two excellent daily newspapers.

Chapter 9
A Journalistic Pot of Gold

Smug new reporter in Louisville, smoking a Kentucky
cancer-causing tobacco product. Unknown photographer.

Shortly after arriving in Louisville, I approached the personnel department of *The Louisville Times* clutching a handful of my editorials, news stories and photos from *The Glenwood Sage*. I asked if they had any job openings available and, indeed, they did. It turned out that *The Times'* daily picture page editor had just left for a job with the *National Geographic*. Good timing. The job was mine.

I worked directly under Norman Isaacs, the newspaper's high-powered managing editor who considered the daily picture page his own personal fiefdom. From "Mr. Isaacs," as I called him, I absorbed his whirlwind method of selecting photos; from the Design Department, I learned how to lay out pages; from the Photographic Department's Bill Strode, who had a gifted eye with a camera, I learned how a crack photographer sees and works. (Bill was named National Press Photographer of the Year in 1966.) And from the reporter John Fetterman, I learned that a writer's humor can make a routine story sparkle. John was assigned to cover groundbreaking for a new Louisville Post Office by President Kennedy. Rather than focus on the need for a new post office, John's front-page story featured a lecture to the young president, instructing him how to use a shovel properly, thus avoiding back pain that had long hounded JFK.

When I became a staff writer for *The Times,* I carried my copy over to the fearsome Copy Desk like everyone else. If your copy was returned for corrections or omissions once or even twice, you would probably be fine, but if it happened more often, beware, because one more error could land you out on the street. Clean copy was expected at *The Times* and the Copy Desk was the great enforcer. This was an excellent learning curve for me.

Our life in Louisville was enhanced when Katy delivered our son Nicholas in the spring of 1961. Nicholas was a delight as well as a handful of energy. His first word was "Glicken," spoken on his grandparent's farm when a chicken cruised by his outdoor playpen. If you ever see "Glicken" on a license plate today, that will be his. The lad is now working in California's dot-com world.

After two years at *The Louisville Times*, I had learned more than I had ever imagined. The newspaper was truly a pot of gold for a new journalist like myself: professional management, a highly skilled staff and a newspaper grounded in the time-tested ethics of fairness and truth in reporting. Despite the advantages of life and work in Louisville, the restless journalist in me needed new challenges, so our little family moved East.

Son Nicholas, born on Derby Day 1961,
at Blackacre, the family farm in Kentucky.

Chapter 10
One of Life's Many Challenges

The poster child for my series on rural poverty
for Middletown Times Herald Record (January 27, 1964).

In Orange County, New York, we rented a weathered house in Goshen, the county seat. I would walk a few minutes downhill to a small office that I shared with my good friend, Jim Ottaway. That was no coincidence. Jim had been my roommate in college and his father was the owner of the very progressive *Middletown Times Herald Record* that installed the first offset press in the U.S. Because of the remarkable ability of that press to reproduce high quality photographs, the *Record* became a magnet for reporters, like myself, who were particularly interested in photojournalism.

As I recall, first there was a period of routine reporting, county commissioners, school boards, elections, etc. Then things began to change. Jim was whisked away to edit a family newspaper in Pennsylvania and I was moved to the *Record*'s headquarters in Middletown where I became more involved in national issues. I was granted two weeks to investigate and photograph the effects of poverty in Orange County. Robert Van Fleet, chief of Ottaway News Service, added to the story by covering President Lyndon Johnson's War on Poverty. It was 1964 and the successful series ran for a week.

A year earlier, I had an experience that changed my life in a way I cannot explain. President Kennedy planned to travel to an estate in rural Pennsylvania to dedicate the Pinchot Institute for Conservation Studies. Although it was outside our circulation area, I felt it important that our staff cover the event, which we did. The President arrived by helicopter from Washington, and was driven up to the Gifford Pinchot house with his Secret Service agents. Soon he set out by himself on a secluded flagstone walkway that led to an outdoor amphitheater where he was to give a speech on the environment. Where was I? Well, for some unknown reason I had dived into a nearby rhododendron thicket, climbed a hill, and come out on the same secluded flagstone walkway that bordered the house. I was alone, except for the man walking toward me. It was the President, also alone. He was relaxed, pleasant. He asked me how I was, then moved toward the amphitheater. Three months later he was shot dead while riding in an open limousine with his wife in Dallas, Texas.

I was deeply affected by this tragedy. First, there was my unexpected meeting with this important but kindly man; then, his untimely death in a Texas motorcade. It seemed to me that life was too short, that I needed to make a radical change in my life.

In the meantime, we had welcomed a new child into our family, a delightful baby, Emily. Katy and I soon purchased a travel trailer, installed a crib for Emily and a bed for Nicholas and parked it at a nearby farm. We moved in to learn the ropes of trailer life. When ready, I left my job and our family headed West.

Daughter Emily, born on June 5, 1963.

President Kennedy signing autographs at the Pinchot Institute
in rural Pennsylvania (September 24, 1963).

Chapter 11
Looking for What Is Next

Heading west in a station wagon pulling our new trailer home.

This was not the first, nor the last time that I headed out into the unknown. "Not knowing" is always an uneasy place to be. You love it, but you want it to be over. Before it's over, you wonder if you made a huge mistake. But when it's over, you kick yourself for having lost your nerve.

Of course, none of this really matters, so one just continues on the path.

We stopped in Kentucky, parked under a shade tree at the family farm for a weekend while my parents soaked up time with their grandchildren. "I really do wish I could go with you," my mother said as we loaded up to drive further West. I know she meant it.

Back on the Open Road, through steamy Missouri and never-ending Kansas, on to Albuquerque, then down to a simple, shaded trailer park on the edge of the Rio Grande River to take stock.

It is easier to tell you where we ended up, rather than trace the circuitous route that got us there – which included a failed attempt to publish a photo story about a young girl trying to start a newspaper in the ghost town of Patagonia, Arizona, as well as my report on a float trip down the Snake River with Lady Bird Johnson and Secretary of the Interior Stewart Udall.

The truth is that I often found it extremely difficult to be a freelance journalist while we were moving. This was before cell phones, thus one needed a fixed base to receive phone messages and mail. My solution? We ended up at a trailer park back in Aspen where I practiced my fence-building skills with a crew consisting of myself and three others, Storrs, Whisper and Brad. I also moonlighted by working on a book about Aspen with Peggy Clifford, a local writer.

It was after fencing work was finished one day that my new world began to take shape. We were sitting in an Aspen grove, passing around a canteen of water when the questions came up. "What are we doing here? Where are we going? What would we rather be doing?" There was a brief period of silence, plus some joking around, then a string of answers. Storrs said he would really like to be a veterinarian, but it would take a lot of medical training. Whisper said he always wanted to be a teacher, but he would have to go to school to get a teaching certificate. Brad, who had worked as a banker on the East Coast, said he liked his life the way it was but was thinking of buying a better truck and maybe moving to Crested Butte. I said that I wasn't sure but thought I might like teaching at the college level.

The following week we were back fencing again, plus we had a new idea: Why not drive over to Boulder together and enroll at University of Colorado? So that fall, we did. Storrs dug into his science courses, Whisper began work toward his teaching credential, and I enrolled in the Journalism School's master's program. By springtime, Storrs had dropped out and had moved to Montana, Whisper was well on his way to his teaching certificate, and I was finishing up my master's thesis about the *Denver Post*'s editorial department. I also had an offer to teach at UCLA in the journalism department's graduate school, which I accepted.

Chapter 12
On to Edgy California

You probably know that L.A. stands for Los Angeles, but I didn't until I moved there. "Can you tell me the name of that large body of water one sees as you circle Los Angeles in an airplane?" That was my whispered question to Bill Johnson at a faculty lunch during my job interview at UCLA. I was sure Bill would know the answer. He was a well-known *Time/Life* reporter, and the only faculty member wearing a work shirt. Bill leaned close, and speaking very quietly, replied, "John, that's the Pacific Ocean." I tell you this so you will know how utterly sophisticated I wasn't before moving to California.

I loved teaching in sunny California. I helped Bill Johnson and Jim Howard with the basic reporting course for all students in our department. I also taught photojournalism and graphics classes plus darkroom work.

When teaching photography, I often sent students out to travel by bus anywhere they wished in the city and return with either photographs or a list of subjects that they hoped to capture on camera someday. A more important assignment was to find a photographer who was working in an area that interested them, such as sports, fashion, portraits, politics, police work, nature, etc. The assignment was to interview the photographer, observe how they worked, and bring in samples of their work to discuss in class. Then the unexpected occurred, shaking me to the core.

It was near the end of the term. We were in a small room with about six students prepared to report their findings. One of the students explained that she was interested in portrait photography. She had interviewed a highly respected artist who photographed individuals he admired and had gotten to know over a long period of time. The student then passed the first portrait around the table. When it came to me, I held the print and was face to face with a life-size image of my grandfather who had died several years earlier and was now looking directly at me.

My grandfather, John Henry Strong,
photographed by his daughter Elizabeth.

Quite honestly, I was in shock and unable to explain to the class what had just happened to me. I could not talk about this incident for years without choking up. On reflection, I was amazed by how deeply I was affected by my grandfather's sudden "presence." I had loved and admired him and was named for him, but until that moment, I had no awareness how much he had meant to me. In my emotional paralysis, I was somehow able to dismiss the class, but unable to ask the name of the photographer. I regret not being able to talk to him about my grandfather or at least order a copy of his portrait. At that time, I had no ability to reveal my personal emotions in the classroom.

Now a question: Was my unexpected meeting with my grandfather's portrait simply an extremely odd coincidence, or was it something more? I don't have the answer, but it does make me wonder. And the following story makes me wonder even more.

For no reason that I could imagine, I was invited to a weekend student retreat at a mountain resort in Southern California named Big Bear. We were traveling there to discuss "Alienation," a subject that was totally lost on me. We arrived by bus, and I was shown to a room and told that I had 15 minutes before I was to speak to a group of students in a nearby meeting room. A few minutes later, a charismatic young priest from LA entered, shook my hand, told me he unfortunately needed to return immediately to his parish and would not be able to participate in the event. It was beginning to look like I was set up for failure. What to do? Well, if my departed grandfather, a Baptist minister, had been trying to reach out to me in my classroom, why not send him a distress call about my "Alienation" assignment? So, with less than ten minutes to go, I walked out to a nearby courtyard and paced the flagstones while sending a message to John Henry Strong. "Grandpa, you're the preacher, not me, and I need your help right now! I have just a few minutes before I have to talk to some students about Alienation, something I know nothing about. For heaven's sake, send help, I need inspiration!"

Just then a facilitator came out and showed me to the door of a modest-sized meeting room. Inside, college students were sitting on the floor. They seemed relaxed, cheerful. I told them that I really didn't know anything about "Alienation", but I used to work on a farm in Kentucky. I described how one mows hay in big circles from the outside inward and how when the tractor and the cutting bar get closer and closer to the center, all the little animals that have been moving inward to avoid the life threatening cutter bar are facing sudden death. So, I asked the students what they would do if they were driving the tractor. Answer: Sometimes it is a good idea to stop what you are doing and go have a cup of coffee, or a beer. Little creatures will thank you for it. (Laughter.)

I continued by reporting that a red fox had been killing our chickens one winter and I had been selected to hunt him down. On a lower field, I discovered some steam coming out of a frosty hole in the ground. "Ah, ha! I have found the fox in his lair breathing telltale moist air out the mouth of his den." Summoning help, we built a fire in the mouth of the den to smoke out the fox. No dice. The moist air persisted. We realized it wasn't fox-breath coming out of the hole, it was actually the warmer air from the ground entering the freezing atmosphere outside. After lots of effort for no return, I learned that sometimes things are not what they appear to be. (Groan.)

Things went fairly rapidly until my time was up. I had dished up more farm stories, and my grandfather seemed to have rescued me with the concept of parables, and the audience seemed to love it. I was both puzzled and amazed.

At that time the UCLA campus, as well as our department, was deeply consumed by the war in Vietnam. (It was actually *our* war!) This was 1970 when campuses throughout the U.S. were protesting both our government's role in the war plus the killing of unarmed, protesting students at Kent State by Ohio's National Guard. At UCLA students were on strike, classes were cancelled, the campus was closed down and armed police occupied the rooftops.

What to do? I had recently met a young couple who had demonstrated a keen grasp of Vietnam's history. I had no idea if they were actually students, but they agreed to talk at public meetings if I took care of the arrangements. Our first meeting was in the boardroom of a Westwood bank. There were only about 25 people present, but they showed interest in learning about Vietnam's history.

For our very last engagement, I took a chance and called the Rand Corporation in Santa Monica, a "think tank" that played an important role in the destructive war due to its close connection to the U.S. government. I was surprised that Rand agreed to let us in the door and even more pleased at the turnout that evening.

As I recall, we met on the ground floor of the Rand building, in a spacious room near the main entrance. There were no chairs, so it was standing room only and the space was full. Our little group talked about the war and the history of Vietnam. At the end of our presentation, I asked if there were any questions. There were no questions or comments, but from the back of the room came a single, very loud, clear voice that said: I AGREE WITH EVERYTHING YOU HAVE SAID TONIGHT!

A documentary about the Pentagon Papers.

Years later I was surprised to hear that same clear voice again, this time on the radio. It was the voice of Daniel Ellsberg, testifying before Congress. When we heard him for the first time in California, he was probably still in the process of removing copies of The Pentagon Papers from the files at Rand Corporation.

Ellsberg, a man of conscience, risked prosecution and jail by turning over 7,000 pages of Top Secret government reports, including presidential lies, to the press. His action led to Watergate, President Nixon's resignation and the end of the Vietnam War.

Ronald Reagan was Governor of California at this time. He was also in charge of the entire University of California education system. Reagan's budget axe came down swiftly on all the university campuses due to student anti-war protests. Journalism was particularly targeted because it was the carrier of "all the bad news" of the Vietnam War.

A memo to our faculty from Department Chairman Walter Wilcox began with the words, "We are doomed!" Realizing that the future of the department was soon to be on life support, I decided that I would prefer to leave the university after five good years and seek new challenges rather than face my other option. And that was? Years of frustration working toward a Ph.D. required if I were to continue teaching in graduate school. It was an easy choice for me.

Nicholas and Emily eating lunch at home in the Santa Monica Mountains.

Chapter 13
Trying Something New

When leaving California I took two new tools. The first was an idea. I had recently written an academic paper about the lack of community access in television programing. I was thinking particularly about Watts, a neighborhood in South Central Los Angeles, as well as small rural towns everywhere. These areas receive television news from major cities with little input from smaller communities or local residents.

In Los Angeles I had purchased a small, newly developed portable video camera and recorder using half-inch, black and white videotape. My plan was to see if I could create a community cable casting station in a small town using the new video camera for public access. I described my plan to a good friend who operated a television station in Louisville. He listened politely, thought for a moment, then delivered his one word assessment: "Impossible!" That was exactly what I wanted to hear. Nothing is more motivating than to be told that something is impossible.

My wife and I packed up our two children and pets and headed to Colorado where, during the summer months, we had been building a cabin on an old ranch up Little Woody Creek, a few miles downstream of Aspen. In my view, Aspen was the perfect community to try out something that had never before been done. (Full disclosure: I later learned that one community in the U.S., Austin, Texas, had received non-profit status for community television but had never launched a station.)

Back in 1971, when GrassRoots was founded, Aspen was a vibrant community. People knew their neighbors, real estate was affordable, the residents were very aware of the town's mining history, and eccentricity was almost a requirement for residency. That changed in 1978 when 20th Century Fox purchased Aspen Mountain with its Star Wars' earnings, and Hollywood started to move in. Neighborhoods, once populated with children, pups, and ponies, soon became deserted, except at Christmas and other holidays when out-of-towners flew in.

In the early 1970s, Aspen had a ton of local talent and city and county administrations that were open to new ideas for the community. Neither Katy nor I were new to Aspen. Katy had taught Math in Aspen's public school system, I had worked for Bil Dunaway at *The*

Aspen Times and his other weekly, *The Glenwood Sage*. I had also worked on a book about Aspen with local writer Peggy Clifford. Although we lived down river, the town of Aspen was very familiar to us and seemed like a perfect place to launch an experiment like GrassRoots.

What I didn't know, of course, was anything about television, cablecasting, operating a video camera or managing volunteers and raising funds to support a non-profit foundation. All that came with the job.

GrassRoots' first volunteer was Eleanor Bingham, from Louisville, with no prior experience, but eager to learn about media work. Our first phone call was from a young electrical engineer named David Wright who said, quite accurately: "You need me!" "Tell us where you are and we will be right over," I replied. When we found his "doublewide" in the Smuggler Trailer Court, David got right down to business. "First you need a modulator." "*A What?*" "A modulator, it's a black box." Our first donation was from Bil Dunaway of *The Aspen Times*, for a modulator. "Second, you need to get a channel on the cable." That was no problem since we would be providing free public service programing for the cable company. Channel 12 became ours. "Third, you will need a transmission base and you can use my trailer, if needed." We accepted David's kind offer, and transmitted from David's trailer until we convinced the local cable company to give us the use of their studio.

David Wright was an engineer and a genius. He was also a very generous fellow. He basically set up our station, showed us how to edit our weekly programs and transmit them to the local cable system. He also repaired our system when it failed.

Meanwhile, the city had given us office space in the Wheeler Opera House, the county had given us a grant, and we had become a non-profit corporation with a board of directors. We were finally launched, and it was not long before we were discovered by the outside world. Highly capable people like Candy Harper, Linda Maslow, Randy Bean, Dan Hindelang and many others found their way to our door to become prime movers in the station's development.

Family life up Little Woody Creek with lots of kids and animals.

Nicholas and Emily in Little Woody.

Chapter 14
The Smash Hit That Launched Us

While visiting *The Aspen Times* one morning, a young reporter named Sally Barlow asked me if GrassRoots could produce a soap opera about Aspen. The next issue of the Times carried a small item asking anyone interested in the idea to meet at David Michael's house at 7 p.m. that Saturday.

At 6 p.m. on Saturday, there was no more room to park at David's. At 7 p.m. David's house was so full of people it was standing room only. Everyone seemed to be talking at once about the history of the town, what the plot of the soap opera should be, who should star, who would write the script, when to start, where to rehearse, etc.

Tryouts for actors were held in the Wheeler Opera House the next day. Writers gathered to work on the script; rehearsals were scheduled; episodes were shot on videotape every weekend throughout that first summer and shown daily on Channel 12. Cable subscribers had dinner parties for residents without cable to watch the weekly productions of *The Edge of Ajax.* (Ajax being the old name for Aspen Mountain.)

I know that you have been waiting for a summary of the soap opera. Here it is, accompanied by local church organist Elmira Snyder.

ANNOUNCER: Presenting . . . THE EDGE OF AJAX.
[Organ Swell]

A contemporary drama about the world of Felicia A. Wheeler of the Roaring Fork Valley.

Felicia's Origin is shrouded in mystery. She was found as an infant, wrapped in beaver skins and tied to a dog sled in the dead of winter on top of West Maroon Pass. Brought to Aspen and raised by the local jailer, Felicia was named after one of Aspen's early pioneers, Jerome B. Felicia. After being sent off to school in the East, Felicia eventually married Monroe T. Wirthwell, a wealthy land developer. Felicia is now divorced and back in the Roaring Fork Valley with her two children, trying to cope with modern day Aspen and solve the mystery of her own identity!

Producers from Hollywood heard about the project and wanted part of the action, as did notables from Aspen and beyond. GrassRoots was on the map and the rest is history.

GrassRoots quickly grew into a popular training ground for people interested in television. We mailed letters to colleges throughout the U.S. inviting students to apply for internships. We selected the most promising applicants, welcomed them to Aspen and suggested they start by designing, then producing, a program for GrassRoots. It was genuine on-the-job training, and it soon qualified for federal support under CETA (Citizens Educational Training Agency). Our stars at Grass-Roots often went on to much greater things in the media world, Eleanor Bingham producing documentary films, Linda Maslow launching her own media company in Washington, D.C., Dan Hindelang operating cable companies in Costa Rica, Randy Bean doing video for Stanford University, Candy Harper teaching communications on the East Coast. Andy Stone's first news show for GrassRoots disclosed area phone tapping by the Nixon Administration. He now heads *The Aspen Times*. I could continue, but my memory says no.

Hippy journalist watches GrassRoots grow.

Chapter 15
Confronting the Unknown

Some people believe they can see at least a few weeks or months ahead in their lives, but the truth is, one never really knows what is in store for us. So it was for me in the summer of 1978. I was alone in our cabin when I received a phone call from a person I barely knew. She said she needed to talk to me "right now." She then described her situation to me. I do not recall the details of our conversation, nor do I remember my exact response. The gist of what I told her was to consider launching a new chapter in her life. After our talk, she thanked me and hung up the phone. Years later, when I was living in another state, that woman somehow reached me by phone and thanked me for "changing her life," as she put it. I now wonder if that woman's call for help hadn't been a glimpse into my own future.

Not long after that woman's original call, I had driven to the Aspen hospital to visit Katy and confer with our family doctor. The doctor told me that Katy, who had fallen in love with a local artist, was heavily sedated and suicidal. He explained neither Katy nor the artist seemed capable of making a decision about their lives. He asked me if I could make a decision that might resolve the situation and perhaps save Katy's life.

I recalled a question that my grandfather had once asked me when I was a child. It was a question I had never before been able to answer. "If you were in a raging river with a family member," he asked, "and there is only one rock in the river that could save only one person, what would you do?" Years after my grandfather's life was over, I finally had the answer.

I returned home, packed up my truck, kissed my remarkable children goodbye, loaded up my dog Ajax and drove off into the unknown.

It was almost dark a day later when I stopped near the end of a dirt road in the middle of nowhere. I got out of the truck, fetched some water for Ajax and walked over to a small sign posted at a barricade in western Utah. It read Muley Point. I peered over the barrier, and saw what I can only describe as the End of The World, The Abyss.

At dawn the next morning, I walked along the dirt road and picked up a tiny, white quartz arrowhead. The tip was bright red. "Ah, the Universe Speaks," I said to myself. It felt like I had just jumped out of an airplane without a parachute.

Before I begin the story of "my new life," it might be useful to mention one personal experience that stands out as I look back at my time at GrassRoots. It was my experiment with "the problem of burnout."

Naturally, there were occasional staff issues at GrassRoots, plus board issues, equipment problems, scheduling conflicts, First Amendment clashes, and funding worries, to mentions a few. At one point, I discovered that my head was not only spinning but seemed to be boiling over. I could not slow down nor have quiet time being alone. I had become a living, whirling dervish, without the divine part.

My solution? I decided to seek total solitude and see if that would cure me. I took a canister of water, a few apples and oranges, some raisins and a sleeping bag, and drove west in our VW van. It was almost dusk when I came to a remote spot in neighboring Utah where I felt I would be undisturbed. I parked, lifted out my knapsack and followed a small trail bordering a stream. I plodded along slowly, like an old man dragging a heavy sled.

When darkness settled in, I stopped, pulled out my sleeping bag and laid it on the ground close to the moving water, hoping the sound would calm my frayed nerves and send me off to sleep. It didn't work. To my ears, the sound of the moving water became unfamiliar voices in endless, heated debates about nothing I could understand. I tried shouting at the voices, but that didn't work. Finally, fatigue won out and I slept until dawn.

In the morning, I left my pack and sleeping bag near the creek and carried my water jug and fruit to climb up and investigate the slick rock on the canyon's side. For hours I sat in the sun on the edge of a gigantic rock bowl. I wondered where the indigenous peoples had worked their flint arrowheads and spears and where they had left their stone tools. It was high noon when I finally realized that what I was looking for was right in front of me. Tools were scattered all over the rocks below. I simply did not have the eyes to see them.

In the afternoon, the sun's heat told me it was time to move on, so I climbed higher, up to the cooling shade under the rock overhang near the top of the canyon. The rest of the afternoon I sat there in the shade on a soft mound of earth. And what was I doing? I was pondering where the arrowhead makers moved after they, too, felt the heat of the afternoon sun. And it didn't take long for me to look more closely where I was sitting. It didn't appear to be an adobe wall, but it certainly had been centuries ago. Weather and time had eroded the walls of the dwelling into soft mounds of earth making a pleasant place for me wait out the sun.

I returned to the stream at sunset, took a quick dip in the cool water and then sat on the bank to finish my last apple. I fell into a deep sleep on my bag. The voices in my head had all disappeared.

I was up before the sun in the morning. I packed up my bag and moved out with a light step. I was happy, heading home and back to work. Burnout had met its match in solitude, and I was no longer afraid to be alone. This was fortunate, indeed, because now, many months later, I found myself at Muley Point without a parachute.

A selfie taken after a desert trip to cure overload, including a therapeutic dunk into the Escalante River.

Chapter 16
The Lost and Found Years

Ajax: The King of Dogs.

Where to go? I headed back to California where our family had previously lived. We had friends up one of the canyons in the Santa Monica Mountains, so Ajax and I drove there and found a small rustic cabin for rent that was perfect. Ajax and I moved in.

Fast-forward a month. I had placed cards on local mailboxes announcing the arrival of Celestial Maintenance, my new occupation as a handyman, featuring "Expert Knife Sharpening, Peerless Window Washing, Fearless Trucking & Hauling, Letter Writing Services and more." The card was signed "John Smith, since 1933" (my birth year). Business picked up slowly, and so did I.

This was an extremely painful period for me. So many losses, so quickly. My family, friends, the talented GrassRoots crew, the mountains, plus an end to the most interesting and challenging job I had ever had, creating the country's first community cablecasting station.

There are many ways that people cope with pain. There are drugs, alcohol, shopping, abusing oneself, becoming violent, or simply being nasty and blaming others for one's own misery. My solution was this: I would live with the pain for as many days as I could, then I would "take a brief vacation" with a beer and maybe a joint. That would give me relief for a short period, perhaps one day. I would then rejoin my pain until it again became too much of a burden. I was fully aware of the danger of addiction, and I could see how someone might prefer a life without any pain at all. But I made sure that addiction was not going to be my middle name. By giving up my drugs of choice when they were no longer needed.

Using my handy truck and my wood working tools, I kept busy with light home repair jobs and dump runs. My knife sharpening skills found work in a local restaurant and I also did a project for a film company researching documentary possibilities in the West – an offshoot of *Aspen Dreams and Dilemmas*, the book that Peggy Clifford and I had published years earlier.

Most important of all, the two years after leaving Colorado, which I call my "Lost and Found Years," turned out to be a valuable period of personal growth for me. I credit three things that made my transformation possible. First, I was never lonely because I had the steady, dependable companionship of Ajax, the king of all Golden Retrievers. Second, I was in almost daily written contact with a wise man named Harper Brown who basically helped me reset my internal hard drive. (You will learn more about Harper later.) And the third factor that moved me forward? I gave up the cabin and moved onto an old wooden sailboat to become a budding saltwater sailor. The boat was moored at Channel Islands Marina near Oxnard.

I now interrupt this sequence to report a significant moment in my transition from Lost to Found. I do not recall the year, but I was alone, standing on the beach with the Pacific Ocean at my back and the hills of Santa Monica before me. It was Christmas Day, shortly after I had flown with Ajax to visit my parents on the family farm in Kentucky. On our first morning there, Ajax and I were exploring the hills and pastures when I suddenly realized Ajax was not by my side. This had never happened before. I called for him and then began searching for him. I found his body near the stream. I carried him up the hill to the house, dug a hole near the house, placed Ajax gently in the ground and shoveled the soft earth over him. I had just lost an irreplaceable companion who had saved me more than once by barking me down from my own folly when I was rock climbing. Ajax, who I occasionally referred to as "my better self," actually seemed to know me better than I did.

That Christmas day standing on the beach in Santa Monica, I looked up and realized that all the dwellings above me were filled with housebound families. I was standing alone in the universe, yet entirely free and finally capable of continuing on without Ajax.

And with my new outlook on life came my new perspective about Celestial Maintenance.

Business card announcing my new directions, at last!

Chapter 17
The ABCs of Celestial Maintenance

We live on a green, watery planet called Earth. The Earth is one tiny speck in a universe of trillions of dry, perhaps lifeless stars.

Each of us has been given life and a life-kit on this planet for a limited amount of time. Our life-kit consists of our body, our consciousness, our special identity, and our own individual fortune-cookie assignment.

Collectively, what we choose to do with our time here on Earth is written as the History of the World.

Individually, what each of us does with our time here, our actions as well as our words, affects first ourselves; second, others; third, the planet; and, last but not least, the universe itself.

Celestial Maintenance gets its authority from the fact that every action we take affects the universe. In fact, you and I have been involved in Celestial Maintenance since birth.

Each of us is maintaining the universe at this very moment. By simply breathing and pumping our hearts, we are maintaining life on this planet.

And now for our individual fortune-cookie assignment: First, the closest, easiest and most important thing we have to maintain is that over which we have the most knowledge, contact and control: ourselves. Each of us knows what is best for us and we must take full responsibility for our physical and mental-wellbeing. By maintaining ourselves to the best of our ability, we earn our merit badge from Celestial Maintenance, and by also assisting others when needed, we can add lightness to our step.

My mother's pot of flowers at the family farm.

Chapter 18
How To Find What You Were Not Looking For

Each of us develops our own system of navigation, whether we realize it or not. Personal navigation was far from my mind until I suddenly realized how valuable it has been in my own life. I'll give you a few examples, then you can decide if it is a worthwhile subject for you to explore.

Back home in my Colorado days, I had once found myself staring at a road map, specifically at a section of coastal California that I had never before visited. It wasn't the coast or any town that I was drawn to, but a non-descript road that traveled away from the ocean and into the hills. The destination made no sense to me at all, but I was convinced that I needed to travel there. So, accompanied by my wife Katy, we packed bicycles into our VW bus and drove 1000 miles to Carmel Valley for three days of uneventful bike touring followed by the long drive home.

After a month back in Colorado, I again pulled out the road map, with the same result. I was drawn to that same stretch of road in California and I knew that I must go all the way back and do that trip again, this time alone. Is this rational behavior? Does it make any sense? Absolutely not, but I did it anyway. And it changed my life.

This solo trip would be different from my previous trip. No planning where to stop or when to eat or when to head home. Just leave everything to fate. It was an uneasy trip with some strange events not worthy of mention. I will spare you the earlier details of this outing and begin with my last day. I had spent a restless night in a sleeping bag atop a picnic table in a high, remote mountain park. Just before dawn, I was hit by a sudden feeling of danger, which was rare for me. I scooted off the picnic table, loaded up my bike and as the dawn was breaking I fled down the hill toward the shopping center where I had started my journey. (Before driving back to Colorado, I asked a gas station attendant about the mountain park where I had spent the night. "One or two murders up there," he replied.)

At the beginning of my bicycle journey I had noticed an old wooden building on the far side of the road. It had a sign for coffee and donuts and I had planned to stop there on my return.

When I reached this coffee house at the end of my journey, the sun was already up. I locked my bike to a fence and went inside. I ordered a cup of coffee plus a sweet roll from the lady at the counter and found a table near a window. A group of older people was chatting at the far end of the room, occasional laughter. Soon they shoved back their chairs and headed for the door – except for a white haired man who approached my table. He asked if I was a local or a traveler. "A traveler," I replied. And would I like a tour of the area? "Yes, I would." That is how I met Harper Brown, the woolly savant who changed my life.

How do you describe a person who "changed your life?" It's probably impossible. But I owe you at least a stab at it. Harper was a brilliant character who traveled "under the radar." He did not pursue fame or fortune and one could probably describe him as a mystic. Harper's own words describe him better than I can.

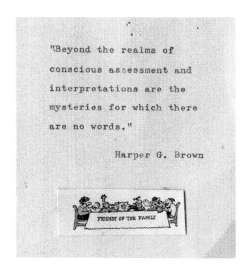

"Beyond the realms of conscious assessment and interpretations are the mysteries for which there are no words."

Harper G. Brown

Why did I meet Harper Brown? A friend told me, "It was simply coincidence." But why was I interested in that remote valley in the first place, and why did I have to go all the way back again to find what I didn't know I was looking for? And where was Harper Brown the first time I made that journey, and why was he there the second time? And what if I had not had that "fright" in the campground that got me up early that morning to arrive at the coffee shop just as he was leaving? The answers don't really matter, of course, but the questions do. And what does any of this have to do with Navigating? Is the answer either Everything or, in the case of coincidence, Nothing? And the questions, are those "the mysteries for which there are no words"?

Leonard Epstein, a good friend and a brilliant teacher, knew Harper well and wrote this shortly after Harper died in 1985.

"Harper's mind was open to all wisdom, ancient and modern, East and West; from Freud, Adler, Jung and Reich to Lao-Tze and Zen. And yet he knew that life itself was the great teacher, and finally, in his mastery he was never out of that state of profound meditation on life. Harper never insisted on How or Why, never gave advice. He just illuminated what was. He made us feel good about ourselves and accept the Yin-Yang of our lives. He was unlike any teacher I have known."

As I remember it, Harper seldom asked me questions, but I do recall one time when he did. I had signed up for an Emergency First Aid course in a California coastal town. Harper asked me how I had learned about the course. I was slightly embarrassed to admit that I had been reading the local paper and the notice of the course "just jumped out at me." Harper did not reply. I had a feeling that he was satisfied with my navigation system.

Harper and I corresponded almost daily for almost a decade. He died at the age of 78. The evening of his death Harper was at home in Carmel, California, filling the honey pot for his wife Eve. I was 600 miles away in Oregon, walking in the dark along snowy Battle Creek Road, maybe a mile from home. I am still aware of the exact spot where I suddenly stopped in my tracks, totally conscious of the unseen "presence" of Harper Brown. I called out his name once, waited, puzzled, and then continued walking home. The next morning I received a call from Harper's wife Eve in Carmel Valley saying that Harper had died the night before, at the same time of my walk in the snow.

It is difficult for me to either understand or explain how Harper changed my life. He had been a teacher, a writer, an artist, a journalist, a poet, and, perhaps, something of a shaman. Early on Harper had devoted his life to "rolling away the stones that individuals pile up in their lives which prevent their true being to thrive." In his first postcard to me, Harper wrote, "In the coffee shop, I saw your lantern lit, but thought I could make it shine a little brighter." Harper accomplished this with many individuals in his lifetime. I was indeed fortunate to have been one of them.

Chapter 19
More on Navigation

My sailboat Orion became a peerless teacher for me.
Photographed by Stella Snead in Newport, Oregon.

Earlier in this narrative I mentioned that I left my cabin in the hills of LA for an old wooded boat. Here is the story about that transition. It's the weekend in LA and I am off duty. Celestial Maintenance is going well and I am planning to drive south down the coast. I arrive at the Coast Highway, prepared to turn left, but, strangely, I turn right instead. This is weird, I say to myself, why am I heading North? Soon I am entering Oxnard, "Ox Yard," as our friend Bruce Klepinger calls it. Now I'm approaching Ventura, I spot a campground and camp out. I wake up in the morning, get some breakfast nearby, and hear myself announce to no one that I'm going to that marina and buy a boat. "This is Nuts!" I say to myself. I have never owned a boat, have never considered buying a boat, and wouldn't know what to do with a boat. Nevertheless, I drive a mile down the road, pull into the parking lot and spot an old wooden boat with a *For Sale* sign attached to her rigging. I talk to the man in the office and learn she was home-built by a telephone lineman named John Boatwright. The old gasoline engine on board is not dependable, but the mahogany hull is tight. There have been no offers yet. And, "Yes, you can live aboard if you wish."

The next morning, I woke up in my cabin wondering if I had gone crazy to consider buying a boat. Then another thought came to me: If it's a crazy idea, at least it's not a Really Bad kind of crazy! So I got a loan, bought the boat, gave up the rustic cabin and moved aboard Orion.

Orion did not have "standing room. When I was below deck and stood up, my head and shoulders were outside the main hatch in the open air. I could thus see 360 degrees around me as well as the full night sky – and that moment of wonder found its way into this poem.

61

AWE and WONDER

What is it that draws me out into the night
away from the warmth of cabin and candlelight?
What is it that pulls me out into the icy air
to stand alone and stare
at a starry universe so vast
that my mind is confounded
by dimensions far beyond its grasp?

This pull, this force, is like a silent voice
asking to be heard by a part of myself
too long neglected.
Shivering, I turn to go below,
knowing that I will be unable to forget,
knowing that I will never be the same,
knowing that always within my reach
is the realm where awe and mystery collide.

The purchase of Orion was one of the most, if not *the* most, important development of my adult life! That could be a slight exaggeration, but it certainly beat graduate school. Living on a boat puts you right in the middle of the natural world, aware of every change in the wind and the tides.

It wasn't long before I pulled out the rusty gas engine giving me more room but also requiring me to "single-hand" the boat without power. That made docking down wind a bit complicated. To slow the three-ton boat, I had to abandon the tiller, leap forward onto the raised deck, pull down the mainsail, then jump off the boat and race down the dock to get in front of the moving vessel, grab the bowsprit and slow the heavy tub to a stop before it turned the dock into splinters. It was exhilarating exercise to say the least.

I also learned the skills necessary to sail and maintain a wooden boat. Sanding, painting and varnishing, anchor chains, pulleys, lines, struts, sails, guy wires, navigation, anchoring. The list is endless. Moving onboard also got me moving north, eventually to Oregon.

Chapter 20
New Horizons

One evening I found myself in downtown Santa Barbara peering in the window of a building on State Street. A friend from my previous life in Colorado had offered me a job as a bartender at this location, but looking in the window, it appeared the establishment had been closed for decades. A pair of empty beer bottles sat close to the edge of an old bar in a dingy, dusty room. Three old photographs hung askew on the darkened walls. Sawdust and a crowbar were on the floor. It was a sad sight indeed. "It will take Bill years to put this place back together," I thought. Then I noticed a note on the door announcing a grand opening in three days.

The floor was swept, bottles removed, pictures straightened. The ancient looking bar was stocked with wine and beer and the kitchen was offering fresh fish and Italian dishes. This was Bill White's artistic creation, an 1890s environment in a downtown building reminiscent of Patagonia or early New Orleans. Customers at the Chase Bar felt they had entered a forgotten time zone. Double French doors opened onto the street, so there was ample sunlight, fresh air, and a full view of Santa Barbara's parade of life.

The Chase was usually a mellow oasis. During my months working at the bar, there was not a single fight or even a drunk. However, one evening there was strange electricity in the air. The waiters were edgy and barked their orders without the usual courtesy. The cook was rattled and had twice walked out of the kitchen with threats of not returning. I was trying hard to preserve my professional demeanor without giving into the nasty feeling in the room. It was clear that the lid was going to blow off soon. Then a table of four men paid their bill and left the restaurant. Instantly, the dark cloud lifted. Until their departure none of us realized that those four men had been poisoning the atmosphere. I have no idea if they were heavy drug dealers or if they had killed someone earlier in the day. The message was clear. Bad people carry their own bad weather around with them and that can infect even the mellowest places.

The other side of that coin is also true. Every bar would benefit from having a romantic Irishman like Patrick as a patron. He was a handsome construction worker who often swung into the Chase as soon as his shift was over. His first order was two draft beers, one to drink, the other to admire. After the first beer, he would amble into the small bathroom by the back door to wash up and get generous hunks of plaster out of his work clothes. After the second beer, he would begin reciting poems, his own.

One Sunday afternoon Patrick appeared with a girlfriend. The two of them ordered beers and started popping quarters into the jukebox. Bill had loaded that machine with every old favorite in the book: songs by Edith Piaf, Frank Sinatra, Eartha Kitt, Billy Holiday, Marlene Dietrich, even The Great Caruso. As the sunny afternoon wore on, Patrick and his girlfriend sipped their beers, and in the most unoffending way, they began to smooch. Soon a couple at the other end of the bar caught the mood and did the same. Then another couple followed, and another. All of them sipping, talking, smooching, caught-up in the spell woven by Patrick and his girl. It was a heartening demonstration of the infectious power of Love.

The best music at the Chase did not, however, come from the jukebox. Three times a week an elderly African American gentleman entered the Chase. Dressed in a dark suit and tie with polished shoes, he went directly to the upright piano in the corner, sat down and began to play. The Chase was often packed on the evenings when Lenny Brooks was scheduled to perform, because his music transformed the place. In his late 70s, Lenny grew up with the Chicago School of Jazz in his hometown. His music spoke to his audience in powerful ways.

When Lenny took a break, he came over to the bar for his usual cup of hot mint tea. He was a fairly short man and always preferred to stand at the bar rather than pull up a stool. Lenny was one of the most impressive individuals I have ever met, and because of that, we seldom spoke except perhaps through our silence. What would you say to someone as personally distinguished as Lenny Brooks? How's it going? Great music tonight, Lenny? How about this fine weather? It just didn't seem right. Like those memorable photographs of Picasso, Lenny had penetrating eyes.

There was one question I very much wanted to ask Lenny, but I never did. I wondered if Lenny somehow knew my question. On his very last day playing at the Chase, he left the piano and walked over to the bar. He stood for a moment, leaned forward and told me exactly what I wanted to know. "I am playing the piano for these people, because my music heals them."

Using the *ABCs of Celestial Maintenance*, you can see how Lenny Brooks qualified for a major merit badge for his years of service at the Chase Bar in Santa Barbara.

Enjoying a talk with "Jonsie," a major street character
in Santa Barbara, outside the Chase Bar.
Photographed by Bill White.

Chapter 21
Life or Death?

A dark forest holds its secrets.

This story troubles me whenever I think about it. Many years ago when I was driving my pickup north on Highway 1, I stopped in the vicinity of Big Sur, California to give a lift to a hitchhiker who was headed up the coast to visit friends. After awhile, when our conversation turned to personal matters, he told me he had been plagued by the urge to commit suicide for a long time. I was shocked by this admission. Our conversation went something like this:

"Really! How would you go about killing yourself?" I asked.

"With a gun," he replied.

"What sort of gun?

"A pistol," he replied.

"Have you ever tried it?"

"What do you mean?"

"Have you ever taken a pistol, put a bullet in it, and put the gun to your head?"

"Why would I do that?" he wanted to know.

"Because you would learn if you were really serious about suicide, or if you really want to live but have been burdened for much of your life with an idea that might never haunt you again."

About that time, he motioned toward a cluster of houses on the right, asked to be dropped off, and thanked me for the lift.

I didn't think about getting his name or phone number, but I have often wished I had – to find out which path he took. Was he still burdened by the idea of suicide or, if not, did he choose life or settle for death? I'll never know the answers, but not knowing still haunts me.

Chapter 22
Life Change in a Large Tent

Although I am not a religious person, I have always been interested in "spiritual events." I love the singing and rich music in the old California Missions and when I spot a revival tent in the South, I can't resist entering to see what is happening inside. One day in Southern California I was walking in Santa Monica and noticed a large white tent pitched in the public park that stretches along the beachfront.

A sign invited anyone and everyone to enter the tent, free of charge, and join an Indian Holy Man in meditation. (Unfortunately, I do not recall the name of this mystic from the East.) I entered the tent and found an empty seat next to a heavy fellow who seemed in distress. The interior of the tent was fairly cool and relaxing, except for my neighbor. He was generating enough nervous energy to power an aircraft carrier, enough to distract me like a bad case of heartburn.

The tent was darkened by this time, so I found it easy to slip out of my seat and find a more restful location a dozen yards away. Later, during a period of chanting, an usher approached my new seat and, strangely, led me back to my original location next to my nervous neighbor. My heartburn returned.

In one of the final events, we were asked to form a line to the holy man, and when we arrived in his presence, he gave each of us a small piece of paper with a name on it. It was a spiritual name for each of us. When I returned to my seat, my steamy companion was already there, but he was different. There was no stress in his body and he no longer emitted explosive tension. And for me, no more heartburn. My seatmate leaned over to talk to me for the first time. He said he was Jewish and all his life he had been filled with hate and fear and tension. He mentioned the name he had been given and told me that as soon as he read it, he was suddenly free of his lifelong pain and suffering. I congratulated him and, when it was time, I left the tent and walked out into the sunlight and over to the pier, amazed at what had just taken place.

I have no idea what sort of transformation my seatmate underwent that morning, or why I was returned to the seat next to him halfway through the event. He told me that he had never been to such a gathering before.

It was suddenly clear to me one's life can change radically in just a few moments.

Chapter 23
Two Worlds of Mental Health

After my bartending experience, I worked at a nearby Santa Barbara non-profit called Sanctuary House, located in a quiet residential neighborhood. The house itself was sturdy, a six bedroom Victorian with high ceilings and a homey feeling that pervaded the structure. It housed about a half dozen adults of varying ages who suffered from some form of mental breakdown. Some of the occupants had been in the California mental health system, others had been sent by their parents. The staff had no professional certification in the mental health world, but we provided a safe, supportive, family-like setting with a healthy diet and an understanding group of helpers. Sanctuary House was basically an alternative to psychiatric hospitalization and it seemed to work.

While I was at Sanctuary House, a friend invited me to lunch at one of California's mental hospitals. At lunch we sat close to a second table, this one occupied by patients. At some point, our conversation was interrupted by a scuffle at the adjoining table. Looking up, I saw two large men holding a young woman who was resisting their efforts to force feed her.

Without thinking, I jumped up and told the men to please let go of the woman, which they did. I then found myself in the awkward position of holding the woman up without any idea of what to do next. At first, the woman's eyes were completely glazed over, totally unfocused. Then her eyes slowly focused on me, the stranger who had appeared out of nowhere. If I had to invent words for her, it would have been something like this: *AND WHO THE HELL ARE YOU?*

I have no recollection of what happened next, except the two orderlies had gone elsewhere, and the woman returned to her seat. I returned to my own table and continued the conversation with my friend.

A week or two later I received a message at Sanctuary House, presumably through some sort of grapevine. It was from the young woman, thanking me for my intervention. That was my only experience with a state mental health facility. Not long afterwards, Governor Ronald Reagan closed down all the state's mental health facilities and sent the residents home to fend for themselves. After that, Sanctuary House was busier than ever with people returning from California's recently closed facilities.

Lest I have given you the impression that I have some hidden ability to "do the right thing" in an emergency, I offer you this bit of evidence to the contrary. A young girl, staying in her room on the third floor at Sanctuary House, had stopped eating and was losing weight. One by one, staff members took turns climbing the stairs and visiting her for over a week, to no avail. I was doing dishes in the kitchen one afternoon when Daya, a dedicated supervisor, asked me if I would go up to the third floor and try to talk the young girl into eating. I climbed the stairs, found her lying on her mattress with a pillow and a blanket. I talked with her for a few hours and made no progress at all. A few days later I was driving north, headed for Oregon.

Chapter 24
Another Right Turn, but Why?

I am not sure what to think about this next story. Although it may not have been a life changing moment, it certainly was *something*. I mention it because it was a sudden change in another person.

A few years after I had moved to Oregon, I was driving home after making repairs to my sailboat on the coast. As I drove through the town of Reedsport, I had the unexpected urge to turn right instead of continue straight ahead toward home. The turn took me to the base of a grass levee, a high earthen dike that protects the town from floodwaters. I pulled over, got out of the car and slowly climbed to the top of the levee, still wondering why I was there instead of driving home.

Then I noticed an old man slouched over, perhaps crippled, making his way slowly up the levee from the other side. He had a dog with him. Curious, I stood there to watch. As the old man approached the top of the levee, I called out to him to ask if his dog might be part coyote. The fellow halted and replied that his dog was indeed part coyote. The two of us talked for quite awhile about several things: dogs, the Umpqua River, and the abandoned fort near the river's mouth where arrowheads can still be found. I learned that he was a Native American who worked in the surrounding forests earning a living as a logger. During our conversation, I couldn't help but notice that the old man's body slowly changed. His back straightened, his head slowly came up and, for the first time, I was able to see the fellow's eyes as he spoke. I had just watched the person in front of me slowly change from a seemingly aged cripple into a strong, healthy-looking young man with inquisitive eyes.

At this point, I became somewhat self-conscious. What am I doing here? What was the meaning of the change in this fellow that had just taken place? These were the questions pulling me back to my original plan of getting home. So, I told this now younger man that I had enjoyed our conversation, but I felt the need to get home before dark.

Driving home I wondered about my right turn and the conversation with the fellow. What was I doing up there on the levee, and why was he also up there? Was it on purpose, and, if so, what purpose? Was it a Harper Brown Message showing me that every one of us has an effect on another when we give them our full attention without asking anything in return? I have many questions but few answers.

Chapter 25
Life Moves On

Crow Farm: A barn, a 100-year old house and eight Oregon acres.
Walking down the driveway is Bruce Klepinger, our trek leader in Nepal
who moved our tents next to each other.
Photographed by Stella Sneed.

A few interesting years rolled by while I lived and worked in the city of Eugene, Oregon. But it was the green countryside that caught my fancy and the time was right. Our family cabin in Colorado had been sold after Katy and I divorced, and it was time for me to reinvest in a home and settle down. Not long after that, I was driving north along Territorial Highway, an old military road named when Oregon was still a territory. On my left, I caught a quick glimpse of a small valley with hay fields but few houses. I quickly turned onto Wolf Creek Road, then a half left onto a graveled lane called Coyote Creek Road. On my right was a weathered barn plus an old Victorian farmhouse painted yellow. A For Sale sign was tacked to the fence. I drove in, talked with the owners, Jack and Estella Ledgerwood, and I bought their eight-acre farm on the spot.

Two years later Jim Ottaway, my good friend and college roommate, offered me an opportunity that I could not refuse, a trip with him to Nepal to reach the Base Camp of Mount Everest, at an elevation of 17,600 feet.

Fast forward to our arrival at the airport in Kathmandu, Nepal. Jim and I took a taxi to the Mala Hotel, checked in and were looking for fellow trekkers who would leave with us the next day for our 31 day Himalayan adventure. Jim spotted a young woman in the lobby, introduced himself, and asked if she was on our trek. Her answer, "Yes." Jim saw me approaching and introduced me to the young woman. I took one look at her, shook her hand, and, flustered, abruptly left for my room. There I found a pencil and in my trip log I wrote two words: "Met Catherine!" Why was I flustered? I had just met this woman for about ten seconds and was suddenly and absolutely aware that my life was about to change completely! How does one know such things? I have no idea!

Valentine with Lil' Bit.
Unknown photographer.

Back in Oregon a year later, Catherine and I welcomed Jim and his wife Mary to Crow Farm, with a handful of well-wishing trekkers from our Nepal adventure. When assembled under our apple tree, Catherine and I became husband and wife.

Our neighbors, Dean and Lisa Livelybrooks, baked our wedding cake but forgot to add sugar. We watched with delight as they replaced the missing ingredient by pouring a jar of honey over the carrot cake, creating a masterpiece and a sweet new recipe.

Tying the knot? Photographed by Stella Snead.

Thirty-five years later, Catherine and I are still at Crow Farm, still happily married, and planning to stay here for the foreseeable future.

And did I mention my karmic relationship with my college roommate Jim Ottaway? Decades earlier, I had caught sight of a divine looking young woman at a college dance miles away. On returning to our "males only" college, I insisted that Jim invite this "Goddess" to dinner and allow me to drive him to her college to ensure that he did not lose his nerve. Like the good friend Jim was, he did as I asked. And, as a good guardian, I watched as Jim and Mary Hyde chatted away the evening over hamburgers (and beer, Jim remembers) until it was time for Jim and me to drive home. Two years later Jim and Mary tied the knot. Following that success, I retired from matchmaking. Fortunately, Jim did not.

Talking with my college roommate on an East Coast dock.
Photographed by Mary Hyde Ottaway.

The Crow Farm Barn with wild iris by Lisa and Dean Livelybrooks.
Watercolor by Ron Rick.

Chapter 26
The Question of Coincidence

To me the world seems to be divided into those who see our lives touched by "Coincidences" and those who see "Something More" at work. When I apply the question of "Coincidence versus Something More" to my life-changing meetings with Harper Brown, and Catherine, as well as a few other unusual events, I find myself leaning toward "Something More." Of course I am also unsure what that "Something More" is, or how it works! For convenience, let's just call those meetings and events, "Mysteries." Meanwhile, here is another mystery for you.

Many years ago, while living at our Oregon farm, I dreamed that I had a son whose name was unfamiliar to me. I struggled to recall the name, and finally realized it was Jedediah, a name that was new to me. Some months later, I entered a bookstore in Jackson Hole, Wyoming where I noticed a book by the historian Dale Morgan about the life of Jedediah Smith. On the first page was his full name, Jedediah Strong Smith. That caught my attention because Strong is my mother's maiden name.

If unfamiliar with the story of Jedediah Smith, I highly recommend reading about him if you are interested in the early exploration of the West. In the words of Dale Morgan, Jedediah was "an authentic American hero." He was the first man to reach California overland from the frontier (on foot, of course) and he traveled more of the West than any other man of his time. He survived three of the worst disasters of the American fur trade, including the Umpqua Massacre of 1828 in which 40 of his men were killed by members of the Kelawatsets Tribe. Jedediah later died alone at age 33 when he encountered a hostile Comanche hunting party on the Santa Fe Trail while seeking water for a team of thirsty oxen.

En route to Wyoming one summer, Catherine and I were spending the night in a remote campground in Eastern Oregon. As we drove in, I noticed only one other camper, a lone cyclist setting up his tent near the entrance. The following morning was chilly, so I walked down to the fellow's site and invited him over for some hot coffee and a muffin.

Here is a bit of our conversation at the campground.

"What are you doing out here in Eastern Oregon?" I asked.

"I'm following the trail of a relative who was a Mountain Man."

"Really? What was his name?"

"Jim Clyman."

"Jim Clyman was the name of the man who sewed up Jedediah Smith after a grizzly bear clawed up his face in 1823."

"That's right! But how do you know about that?"

"We know because we are also on the trail of a relative named Jedediah Smith."

Now more about the trail of Jedediah Smith. In 1828, Jedediah was in a canoe scouting for a safe passage across the Umpqua River when his men were suddenly attacked near what is now the town of Reedsport, Oregon. Jedediah avoided the attackers by diving into the water and escaping to the far shore. He then walked 100 miles north to the British Fort Vancouver on the Columbia River. On his return to the site of the massacre with agents of the British fort, Jedediah would have used the old Indian trail that ran not far from our farm.

After investigating the site of the massacre and meeting with the local tribe, Jedediah hiked across the desert to the Great Salt Lake and arrived only two days late for the annual Rendezvous of trappers and Native Americans. Jedediah had been gone for two years and was presumed dead. His unexpected arrival created a wild celebration.

Reading history is one thing, but how can one's dream reveal the name of a long lost relative from almost two centuries ago? Was this a Coincidence, or Something Else? I have no idea, but one could certainly call it a mystery.

Chapter 27
On to the Great Unknown

As I ease into my "senior years," I do wonder what is ahead for our uneasy world, as well as myself. The world will have to take care of itself, of course, but I have to admit that I am not convinced that everything will work out as smoothly as I would like. In the 2016 Presidential Election, we elected a President who, so far, seems to lack many of the basic human qualities expected of our national leaders: honesty, humility, compassion, and, most important, a desire to serve the best interests of all citizens of this country. I am hoping for a significant correction from our country's present course. However, it is also possible that our present occupant of the White House is the harbinger of a very different, and more frightening era. If this occurs, it must be answered with strong resistance from the voting booth.

As for myself, I lack both the faith and "certainty" that many organized religions offer. Still, I do hope to experience the "hereafter" wherever it leads. If it turns out that I have taken a wrong path, what then? Is it too late to say "Oops?" If that doesn't work, how about, "Do you have an opening for a Jester?"

There is some risk in discussing "other worldly events" that some of us may have experienced in our lives, but I feel it is important to be open and honest about these in case it is useful to those who I leave behind. So, here we go.

First, full disclosure. As I mentioned in my introduction, I have either been blessed or cursed by Curious Events in my lifetime, events that I am unable to explain. My Darth Vader apparition during my Army days is one example, but there are many others. For example, once, while in Kentucky, my body felt suddenly broken for no reason at all. The following day I received a call from a thousand miles away informing me that my nephew, Sam Lord, had just suffered a serious spinal injury from the crash of his hang glider in Wyoming.

How does that work? How can one feel what is going on a thousand miles away?

Once, when I was walking with friends not far from home, I felt there was an arrowhead nearby even though I was not looking for one. I excused myself and went to look in a dry creek bed. There it was lying in the sand, a tiny arrowhead designed to bring down small birds. How can a small, inert piece of flint or agate send out "energy" to a person walking some distance away? It defies logic.

These reports may be sufficient for those who are willing to accept them. But for those who cannot accept such other worldly testimony, I can only say that there are lots of "debunkers" who will agree with you. I found that the only thing that changed my own mind about such things was my own experience.

Chapter 28
Poems from the Ether

Wings over Utah's high desert.

I discovered that the "curious events" that taught me the most were almost impossible to communicate in regular prose. I am definitely not a poet, but it turned out that only poetry was able to communicate the essence of what I had experienced. The first event, below, occurred in Colorado, in the 1970s when I was living in our cabin up Little Woody Creek with my family.

"The Gift" is the name I gave the poem because the experience came to me out of nowhere, for no reason I could think of. Yet it seemed like the most important message I had ever received and it needed to be passed on to others who might benefit from its meaning.

THE GIFT

It was a gift
One moment outside of time.
Awakening on an ordinary day
in the silence and stillness of dawn,
one split second
too small to measure
too large to comprehend.

Can you imagine food so potent
that one grain of rice would nourish you for a week?
Or sound so perfect that one note from a flute
would fill your day with music?

So it was with this moment
that might have been lost to doubt or disbelief
had not its resonance lasted on and on for days.
It had no earthly origin;
the usual senses did not apply.
One astonishing micro-second
in a lifetime of earthly sensation.

One tiny glimpse of the infinite
in a life rooted to this plain.
One small taste of what is ahead
when we shed our bodies
and become a harmonious chord in the universal song.

The Gift deserves a few words of explanation. As accurately as I could portray it, the poem describes the reason that I can talk about "what happens next" with those who are facing the end of life as we know it. My poem experience did tell me that when we leave, we shed our bodies and become free spirits. My experience also told me that the "feeling" that we experience when we depart is as close to "divine" as I have ever experienced in this lifetime, because it involves something beyond our normal senses. What happens to us after that I do not know. That is why I am looking forward to discovering the answer for myself.

■

A Postscript from Harper Brown.
And his last poem.

"Every day of our lives we are given assignments in this Earth School and we will be given the same assignment over and over until we learn what is needed to graduate from that assignment and pass on to the next lesson to be learned. Life is always unfinished, always will be, by its very nature."

POEM for MYSELF

With a heavy pack on my back
I climbed to touch
The tip of the *highest peak*…
Yet, from where I stand
Resting, panting, sad,
I see I am at the *lowest point* of the skies…
Now begins again
The greater climb!

Smooth stones in a California river.

Chapter 29
A Few Words about Religion

As humans, seeking something greater than ourselves is indeed a worthy endeavor. Confusion about religion seems to stem from our failure to realize that there is more than one worthy religion in the world besides our own. Had we been born on another continent or in another family or culture, we might be a Buddhist, a Hindu, or attend a Mosque, Synagogue or Cathedral. One additional consideration: All individuals are not made from the same cookie cutter. Some people are "true believers" from childhood and others may be agnostics or even atheists for a lifetime. Atheists? Yes. Those are people who have faith in their belief that there is no God at all.

My own view? Years ago I had an opportunity to ask Billy Graham a question. My friend Pablo had invited me to a casual gathering with Dr. Graham in an east coast city. I asked the famous preacher how one achieves faith in God. The Reverend Graham was quite clear. "If you read every word in the bible," he told me, "you will have faith in God." So I did as he said. But I ended up with even more questions! Why is God a He? And if He is a he, where is his mother? And if He didn't have a mother, how did he get his start? And if God really created the entire universe in six days, who was counting? And why did it take God so long? And why did he need to rest on the seventh day? And what was there before the universe? And why is God called King and Lord like outdated royalty? Clearly, God must be a Pure Spirit and not a He with whiskers. Those may all be silly questions and ideas, but I do wonder if religion isn't focused more on mythology than reality. The truth is, it really doesn't matter. Religion is probably more like Love than you would think, because thinking doesn't really help us with either one.

Now a moment to visit the subject of Answers. On the table next to me, I have a weighty book of over one thousand pages containing tiny type covering about every question one could ask about Christianity, followed by the answers. It was written in 1886, revised in 1906 and reprinted in 1976. *Systematic Theology* was the work of Baptist theologian Augustus H. Strong, my mother's lofty Grandfather. His massive work is still in use by those wishing to serve as ministers in the Baptist Church. It is a fascinating read for those who hunger for more answers than most mortals can manage.

I have dipped into *Systematic Theology* from time to time, but I am not very systematic. Also, I have found that there are other ways of knowing and have come to believe that you and I may already receive experiences from "beyond" whether we are aware of it or not.

Occasionally I get "message dreams" and you may also. These are worth remembering. I had one such dream during my "Lost Years" after leaving Colorado and my family. I was in a small, open boat on a choppy sea. Sharks were circling, indicating danger. While trying to control the little boat, I noticed that when I put the centerboard down to give the boat more stability and send it straight ahead, the boat would do the opposite. It would go out of control. When I pulled the centerboard up, the boat would go straight again. This was obviously counter-intuitive and my dream was telling me that logic was going to get me nowhere in this unsettling period of my life.

Years later, when my life and internal seas had calmed down, I experienced something that remains one of the great mysteries of my time on this planet. In a dream I had just accomplished something that must have pleased the Dream Elf, like peacefully disarming an angry man, or feeding a runaway dog. I was then confronted with what you might call a close-up, a full frame image of an impeccable, ageless man. I looked closely at his face. He was both young and old and clearly Asian. He spoke directly to me with quiet authority. I recall only one portion of his message. He told me I was "glib," which is occasionally true, and also quite funny. I listened to this man in silence, then woke up.

Who was this fellow? What was this all about? I mentioned this odd event to an old friend who suggested that the next time he appears I should ask him who he is. An interesting idea, of course, but I explained to my friend that in this man's presence I was awe-struck and speechless.

My conclusion? This universe is much richer and more complex than I am capable of understanding.

Chapter 30
Varieties of Human Experience

While in Nepal in 1984, a Brahmin and I were resting in the shade near a holy place on the Bagmati River where pyres are lit to burn corpses of the dead. We had been sitting quietly, discussing nothing, when he broke the silence with this brief message: "All religions are basically the same."

■

I once asked Harper Brown about Jesus. Harper said: "Throughout the ages, John, wise men have appeared on earth from time to time to bring light to our lives in times of darkness."

■

On another day, in another year, I was driving in the Cascades, the volcanic mountains of central Oregon. I had hiked into the Three Sisters Wilderness and stopped at Cougar Hot Springs. Standing nearby was a tall Native American man. I mentioned to him that I was not feeling at all well. He thought a minute, then said, "Go home and throw yourself on the ground!" I thanked him and did exactly that. I drove home, parked the truck and threw myself on the ground as he had instructed. I lay there for a few minutes, then felt totally revived. Mother Nature seemed to have curative powers that we are not aware of.

■

While traveling, I once noticed a church off to the right, so walked over and tried the door. It opened, so I entered and took a seat in the back of the church. There was only one other person in the church. She occupied a pew near the altar and was sobbing uncontrollably. I realized that this was probably the only safe place in her world where she could vent the anguish that burdened her. I waited a bit, then quietly left her alone in the church with her sorrow.

■

On another day I was sitting on a pile of rocks near the bank of an Oregon river. Not far from me, a man was sitting in the sun. We struck up a conversation for a bit, but soon he fell silent. Finally, without turning to me, he told me that he had once shot his dog after he had been drinking. He told me that when his dog was hit, the dog ran right to him for help. It was clear to me that the man had held this story within him for many years and was finally able to tell someone.

■

On the radio I once heard Leonard Bernstein's two cheerful daughters quote their father as saying "Goofiness is next to Godliness."

■

A friend of ours named Jimmy, who would not like to be called a healer, has sung in many choirs and considers Christian sacred music to be "The Fifth Gospel." (Matthew, Mark, Luke and John being the first four.) Here is Jimmy's short list:

Bach: *B Minor Mass, St. Matthew Passion, St. John Passion, Magnificat.*
Beethoven: *9th Symphony, Choral Fantasia, Missa Solemnis.*
Brahms: *German Requiem.*
Lauridsen: *Lux Aeterna.*
Mozart: *Requiem, Great Mass in C Minor.*
Rachmaninoff: *All Night Vigil.*
Schubert: *Mass in E Flat, Mass in A Flat.*

■

Helen Jones, a friend in Louisville, is an Episcopal Priest. Here she paraphrases historian Elaine Pagels: Belief is overrated. In other traditions, belief is not as important as practice. What is important is how you live and share with other people. "These are things I agree with completely," Helen adds.

■

Sister Margaret Graziano, a tireless Nun who worked for decades in our county jail told me " Everyone is Someone!"

■

"I'm not Superstitious, I'm just *Stitious!*" said, John Henry Strong.

And from the late Harper Brown:

That which I have not conceived
Lures me constantly,
And where I have never been
Receives me always;
Into the inexplicable was I born,
And **that** I learned was home;
Others went astray and wandered
Helpless among the known
While I, guided by the Hidden-Real,
Straightaway find, forever,
The impossible!

My mother Emmy, a devoted letter writer, at her desk.

Chapter 31
More Questions!

My father Macauley Smith at home.

Two questions remain. How did I get here, and how do I leave? I arrived here thanks to my parents. My father was very accomplished, a tightly wound man with a brilliant, probably photographic, memory. His early childhood was marred by the death of his father when he was four. Then, a few years later, by the drowning death of his surrogate father, whom he was unable to rescue. These two tragedies affected him deeply. He went on to become an Olympic long distance runner, a lawyer, then for many years a Circuit Court Judge in Louisville, Kentucky. He was a generous man, a friend to many and greatly admired. But he was not an easy father for me. The two of us talked to each other, but we never once had a genuine conversation.

In his later years, my father surprised me by asking if I believed in God. This was a shock because I had never once heard him mention anything at all that touched on religion. I was unable to answer him because I did not really trust how he might respond. Too many slings and arrows in the past! If I had to answer my father now, I would say that I haven't yet met God. And since I only believe what I actually have experienced, I will probably have to wait for Him or Her (or Them) to visit me sometime. Or "vice-a, revers-a," as my Aunt Betsy used to say.

Cooling down: My mother savoring "sippage."
Photographed by Winthrop Allen.

My mother, Emmy, and I are a different story, except that I could not answer her question either, until now. Fortunately, the cautious distance that I had with my father did not exist with my mother. The two of us seemed cut from the same cloth. The youngest of three siblings, Emmy was conceived after the tragic death of

Virginia, a sister who died at age three from cholera. My mother said that early on she knew that her role in her family was to make everyone happy after her little sister's death. So, she did. My mother's father was a minister, her grandfather a Baptist theologian. She said that, as a child, she sat through church twice every Sunday, which was "more than enough for a lifetime." That may be why she seldom went to church, or discussed religion in our household. My mother was, however, definitely a "minister" in her own, quiet way. She was always working to make everything and everyone better.

My mother only asked me one question that I can recall, and until now I could not answer it. She asked me this: "Do you know what you have?" "No." I replied. I now have the answer to my mother's question. I have had a life filled with fine friends, a remarkable family, and a wealth of interesting experiences. I also have a lifetime of stories to tell.

I now have a message for each of you who are reading this. I very much enjoyed writing this for you and it is my hope that you may have found something useful in these pages. It is also my hope that at least some of you will consider following my example by leave behind a record of your thoughts, adventures and personal stories for the benefit of those who come after you. Otherwise, how will anyone ever learn who we were?

Each of us was born to depart, or "tip over" as my mother called it. Emmy, who lived to age 102, told me that the phrase "tipping over" came from the household of her cousin Richard Sewall. Richard's son, Ricky, an observant child, announced at breakfast one morning that his pet bird had "tipped over" with legs in the air.

My age is 85 as I write this and I hope to be around for a few more years, but only the Elves know exactly how long that will be. I do feel it is valuable for each of us who arrive at a certain age to take time to talk with our family and our doctor about what is now called *Dying with Dignity*. It's an important, complex, subject because there exists a legal gap between those two words, Dying and Dignity. Check it out!

Here are my own thoughts about "tipping over." When riding a roller coaster at an amusement park, the car you are riding in slowly climbs the rails upward to the top, then you realize that you are about to plunge straight down hill at breakneck speed. At that moment you have a choice. What choice you might ask? The choice to either cringe in fear against the back of the car as it plunges downward, or move forward and pretend you are steering the car as it drops straight down the track. The choice is either paralyzing fear or the euphoria of being a daredevil at the controls of a speeding car. When I leave the planet I hope I remember to be at the controls, because I am very curious to find out what happens next.

My mother Emmy found clouds an excellent tonic
for life's challenges.

Chapter 32
Last Words

Volleyball high in Colorado.
Photographed by Angela Foster.

In the meantime, Stay Healthy, Breathe Deeply,
And, if you feel "out of sorts," go outside and look at the stars,
or go into the forest. Or throw yourself on the ground
to learn what Mother Nature has for you.
Follow your own path to discover who you are
and what you didn't know you were looking for.

Me? I have had a good life and I will always be closer than you think!

Love from Scruffy Smith in Oregon

With Nicholas and Emily.

Here's looking at you as you make notes
about your life that you want others to remember

Acknowledgements with Grateful Thanks

Joey Blum for his guidance in producing this book.

Chrissy Richards for cover design and layout.
(Lightbox Graphic Design, Salt Lake City)

Carol Bryan, Mar Don, Jim Ottaway, Bessie Blum & **Connie Manz**
for diligent copy editing.

Annette Pfautz for expert digital scanning of photos.
(Dot Dotson's, Eugene)

Stella Sneed (1910 – 2006) for her photographs.
She visited Crow Farm several times after Catherine met the intrepid
English surrealist painter and photographer in the wilds of Ladakh in 1984.

My talented wife **Catherine Smith** for working with photos and text.
She helped wrangle my opus to its conclusion.
Without her, this project would have been composted long ago.

Photographed by Faith Echtermeyer.

When life dishes up maple syrup,
give thanks and lick your plate clean.
Photo by Stella Sneed.

Made in the USA
Columbia, SC
05 November 2019